Colo

A Min.

Susanne F. Fincher

Shambhala
Boulder
2016

Shambhala Publications, Inc.
4720 Walnut Street
Boulder, Colorado 80301
www.shambhala.com

This book is a slightly revised edition of *Coloring Mandalas 2* (Shambhala, 2004).

9 8 7 6 5 4 3 2 1

Printed in Canada

♻This edition is printed on acid-free paper that meets the
American National Standards Institute Z39.48 Standard.
♻Shambhala Publications makes every effort to print on recycled paper.
For more information please visit www.shambhala.com.
Distributed in the United States by Penguin Random House LLC
and in Canada by Random House of Canada Ltd

ISBN 978-1-61180-422-5

Introduction

A mandala is a circular design that grows out of the urge to know oneself and one's place in the cosmos. The womblike structure of a mandala creates a feeling of safety and protection. At the same time, mandalas distill the complex rhythms of the universe—and human consciousness—into patterns that are manageable and comprehensible to human beings. So it is that mandalas reinforce our individuality and also help us relate to the ineffable mysteries that give rise to our existence.

In Eastern traditions, mandalas are used to communicate spiritual realizations and as a way to transmit or teach realization to others. The meditator moves his or her gaze along a prescribed pathway in the mandala in order to discover, access, and integrate particular states of consciousness associated with the symbols in the mandala. Through this interaction, the mandala helps devotees cultivate within themselves qualities such as compassion or wisdom associated with the deity symbolized in the mandala.

Sacred circles are also part of Western cultures. Ancient stone carvings of circular designs found in Denmark suggest reverent observance of the sun and the passage of time. Sacred circles in the Christian tradition include the jewel-toned rose windows prominently placed in Gothic cathedrals (see below). They are mandalas that focus and direct the viewer's attention to a sacred symbol framed in dazzling light. In the Islamic world, complex geometric forms worked in stone or colorful ceramic tile are found near the entrances of Muslim holy places in the Middle East and parts of Asia. The dancing lines weave from center to circumference and remind the viewer that the matrix of all creation is the One, Allah.

Christian rose windows are light-filled mandalas
that ignite an experience of God's presence.

In the Americas, sacred circles are well known to native peoples. Circles filled with a single spiraling line symbolize the face of god for Huichol tribes in Mexico. Navaho peoples of the southwestern United States create circular "dry paintings" for ceremonial or healing purposes. Native peoples of the Great Plains construct medicine wheels using the four directions to convey tribal wisdom about life, relationships, and harmony with nature.

A recurring theme in mandalas is an awareness of the passage of time and the realization that human life is in constant flux and flow. Mandalas are used to find meaning in the ongoing stream of human experience. For example, the ancient Romans believed that the goddess Fortuna presided over a celestial wheel that governed the seasons and the fates of human beings. This Wheel of Fortune helped explain the ups and downs of human life: good and bad luck were determined as the goddess Fortuna turned her wheel.

The notion of life as a cycle of ever-changing experiences is also found in some Eastern mandalas. In the Buddhist tradition, existence is viewed as a repeating cycle of twelve stages encompassing birth, death, and rebirth.

Mandalas created by modern Westerners serve much the same purpose as traditional mandalas: they express our experiences and bring about understanding of ourselves and our place in the scheme of things. Mandalas were of special interest to Carl Jung, the well-known Swiss psychoanalyst. He saw them as evidence of a dynamic urge toward fulfilling one's identity as an individual, a process that he called individuation. According to Jung, this development is guided by the Self, the deep inner source of a pattern of wholeness that propels human beings to fulfill their potential. Jung found that the Self generates a spontaneous desire to create mandalas.

As he worked with his patients in analysis, Jung observed that in the course of this inner work, the various parts of the psyche tend to undergo an ever-shifting balance. Clashes between opposites in the psyche, such as the ego and the unconscious, generate energy that helps to transform conflict into harmony. This growth process may be experienced as stressful and challenging to cherished ideas and beliefs. An urge to create mandalas arises as one of the psyche's natural self-regulating mechanisms for bringing about a sense of balance, order, and well-being. (Indeed, those who create and color mandalas often report feeling more relaxed afterward.)

The American art therapist, Joan Kellogg, in association with the psychiatrist Francisco Di Leo, conceptualized the growth and development of the psyche as an ongoing cycle through twelve stages. Each stage encompasses certain developmental tasks and is characterized by a particular state of consciousness. The twelve stages are experienced many times in the course of a lifetime. Kellogg discovered that these twelve stages are associated with prototypical mandala forms.

In Kellogg's model, called the Archetypal Stages of the Great Round of Mandala (or "the Great Round" for short), the twelve stages comprise a complete cycle of inner growth that begins in formless unconsciousness and unfolds into greater and greater self-awareness and accomplishment. The cycle then transitions to the ending when things naturally fall apart, energy returns to the unconscious and a new cycle begins. The twelve stages of the Great Round are called the Void, Bliss, Labyrinth, Beginning, Target, Dragon Fight, Squaring the Circle, Functioning Ego, Crystallization, Gates of Death, Fragmentation, and Transcendent Ecstasy.

Most stages are initially experienced in normal growth and development. We repeat cycles of the Great Round again and again as we live our lives. With each "visit" to a stage we have an opportunity to consolidate our mastery of the challenges and states of consciousness associated with that stage. We may also clarify our understanding of past experiences there, and resolve unfinished business associated with the stage, thereby releasing bound energy to focus on subsequent stages of the Great Round. (For more on the Great Round, see my book *Creating Mandalas*.)

In this book we will focus on one of the twelve stages of the Great Round: Crystallization (Stage Nine). Crystallization is associated with the completion of a cycle of growth that began in the Void (Stage One). It is the point in the Great Round where growing energy is perfectly fulfilled in a unique creation. Imagine a fully opened rose in a sunny garden, releasing its fragrance as it gently bobs in a summer breeze. This is the feeling of the stage of Crystallization.

Crystallization is a time of reaping rewards and benefits from the work we have performed, of realizing and appreciating our achievements, of resting in the pleasure of having fulfilled a personal creative inspiration. Time seems to slow to a relaxed, enjoyable pace. Crystallization is also a time of significant self-realization when our spiritual being and physical nature balance in harmony.

A profound synthesis is suggested in Crystallization mandalas. The Sri Yantra, a traditional Indian design, may be considered such a mandala (see below). Downward-pointing triangles symbolize Shakti, the female principle representing all that is active and creative. The upward-pointing triangles symbolize

The sacred Sri Yantra is a crystal-like Hindu mandala
representing the creative energies of the universe.

Shiva, the male principle and the essence of absolute consciousness that permeates all reality. In the Hindu tradition, the coming together of these two energies is thought to set in motion all of creation.

The sacred art of the world's great religions includes myriad Crystallization mandalas. Typically, Crystallization mandalas are symmetrical and emphasize the center point. They convey a feeling of balance, harmony, and rest. Paradoxically, they also suggest a pulsing energy. The structure of Crystallization mandalas is based on even numbers greater than four (six, eight, ten, twelve, and so on).

I have chosen to focus on Crystallization mandalas in this book because they embody peace, joy, and fulfillment. Spending time with these mandalas can be relaxing. Coloring them can provide a soothing balance for hectic lifestyles. Interacting with Crystallization mandalas may also help you develop your ability to access a calm state of mind more easily, whenever you choose to. And some of you may look beyond the patterns you see in these mandalas to experience the spiritual energy that inspired them.

Seventy-two mandalas are included because 72 is a sacred number containing within it many combinations of sacred numbers, most notably one (symbol of the One, or God), two (representing the duality of life as in yin/yang, male/female, light/dark), three (God as Father, Son, Holy Spirit; Goddess as Maiden, Mother, Crone), four (as in the four directions and the four elements of earth, air, fire, water), and twelve, the basis of the Great Round (as in twelve apostles, twelve sun signs of the zodiac, and twelve months of the year). Many of the mandalas in this book were inspired by the sacred art of Europe, Asia, and the Middle East. Photos of snowflakes provided a beginning point for several. The visual prayers of great souls inspired others. All were drawn by me after opening sacred space by lighting a candle and sitting for a few minutes in meditation. You might enjoy taking the same steps to prepare for coloring a mandala. Whatever approach you take, your time with these mandalas will be well spent.

Susanne F. Fincher
Atlanta, Georgia
2016

REFERENCES

Bently, W. A. *Snowflakes in Photographs*. Mineola, NY: Dover Publications, 2000.

Copony, Heita. *Mystery of Mandalas*. Wheaton, IL: Theosophical Publishing House, 1989.

Fincher, Susanne F. *Coloring Mandalas: For Insight, Healing, and Self-Expression*. Boston & London: Shambhala Publications, 2000.

———. *Creating Mandalas: For Insight, Healing, and Self-Expression*. Boston & London: Shambhala Publications, 1991.

Jung, Carl G. *The Archetypes and the Collective Unconscious*, 2nd ed. Princeton, NJ: Princeton University Press, 1990.

Kellogg, Joan. *Mandala: Path of Beauty*. Rev. ed. Williamsburg, VA: Privately published, 1997.

Kellogg, Joan, and F. B. DiLeo. "Archetypal Stages of the Great Round of Mandala." *Journal of Religion and Psychical Research* 5 (1982): 38–49.

Kluckhohn, Clyde, and Dorothea Leighton. *The Navaho*. Rev. ed. Garden City, NY: Doubleday & Company, 1962.

Sacred Symbols: Mandala. By the Editors of Thames & Hudson. New York: Thames and Hudson, 1995.

Tucci, Giuseppe. *Theory and Practice of the Mandala*. London: Rider and Company, 1961.

Wilson, Eva. *Diseños Islamicos*. Naucalpan, Mexico: Ediciones G. Gili, 2000.

Zaczek, Iain. *Celtic Design*. New York: Crescent Books, 1995.

MANDALAS FOR COLORING

Mandala 1

Angelic beings dance within the sacred circle of the mandala.

Mandala 2

The ever-changing cycles of life seen in flowers, trees, and celestial seasons seem held in a place of harmony within this mandala.

Mandala 3

The eternal dance of nothingness into form pauses at the stage of Crystallization—a moment of beauty.

Mandala 4

This mandala calls to mind a compass, a crystal, or perhaps a star blazing fervently beyond the limits of the human eye.

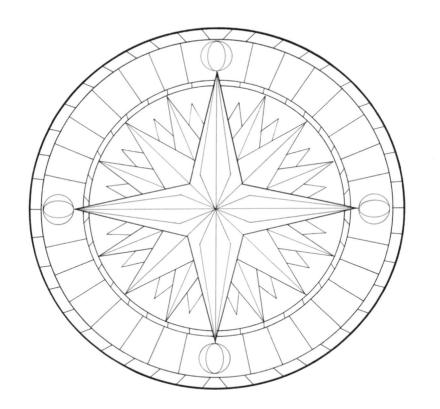

Mandala 5

Six circles intersect, breastlike, nurturing. From deep within comes a voice: "I have all that you need."

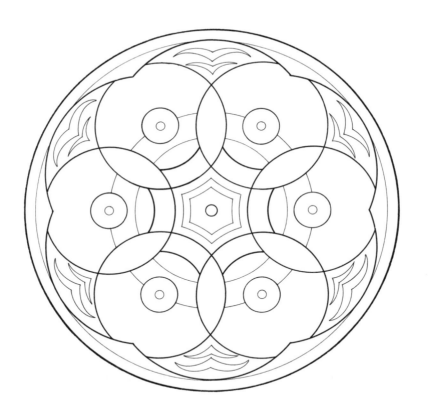

Mandala 6

Rainbows, rising and setting suns, or stars with wings—all enfold the center where an eight-pointed form is crystallized.

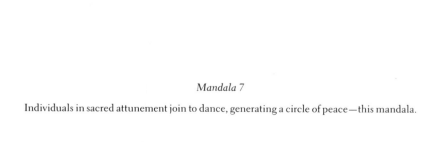

Mandala 7

Individuals in sacred attunement join to dance, generating a circle of peace—this mandala.

Mandala 8

Upward- and downward-pointing triangles rest upon the petals of a fully opened flower, the essence of the stage of Crystallization.

Mandala 9

Layer upon layer of flower petals open around a center that, when left uncolored, suggests a gateway through to changes yet to come.

Mandala 10

Interpenetrating triangles signify the coming together of opposites—dark/light, active/receptive, feeling/thinking.

Mandala 11

Mandalas are all around us, even under our feet, when we take time to notice.

Mandala 12

The crystalline structure of a snowflake was the stimulus for this mandala that blooms like an exotic flower of flowers.

Mandala 13

Dragonflies hover as strange blossoms—each supporting a pearl, or a moon, or a sun—neatly balanced on the tips of a star.

Mandala 14

The intricate patterns of this mandala suggest lit candles, a convivial gathering, or a grove of jeweled trees.

Mandala 15

Resembling a multifaceted jewel, a seal of office, or an honorary medal bestowed for accomplishments, this mandala is based on a snowflake.

Mandala 16

Fanlike forms unfolding evoke the quietly pulsing energy of Life experienced during the stage of Crystallization.

Mandala 18

The rhythms of breath, the opening of a blossom, the sensation of inner peace—all are suggested by this mandala.

Mandala 19

Inspired by the Buddhist Wheel of Life, this mandala alludes to repeating cycles of existence as well as the practice of meditation as a way to break free.

Mandala 20

Contemplative practices mobilize a connection with all those who follow a similar path—communion of saints, sangha, or kindred souls.

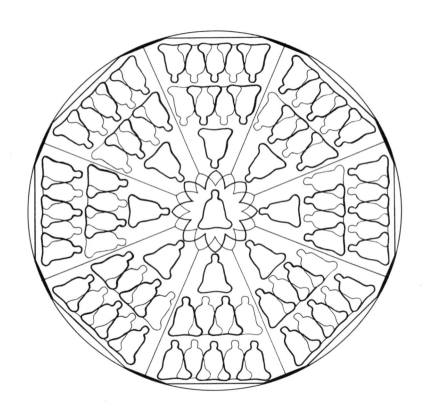

Mandala 21

The rising and setting sun, the waxing and waning moon, or earth energy coursing along lines of natural magnetism: what do you imagine in this mandala?

Mandala 22

A celestial rose supports the form created by two triangles coming together. In the Jewish tradition it is the Star of David, Solomon's Seal, or the symbol of God's union with the Shekhina, the feminine Divine Presence.

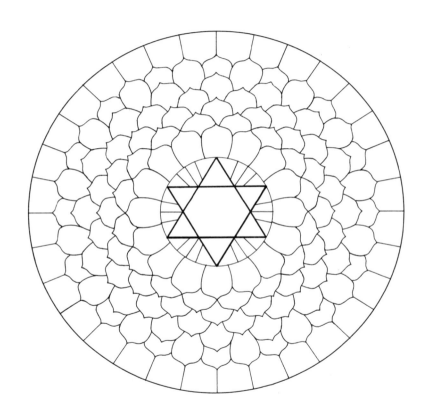

Mandala 23

Lilies drink deep from wafting trails of fragrance linking them one to another. Inspired by the structure of a snowflake.

Mandala 24

Lily buds encircle the center space of this mandala, inviting you to add your own choices of forms and colors.

Mandala 25

The mandalas of Tibetan Buddhism often take the form of a palace or walled city enclosing a sacred inner precinct, as seen in this design.

Mandala 26

Fluffy clouds tug along myriad filaments linked to the center, which stays implacably still, or perhaps even moves in the opposite direction.

Mandala 27

Star-gazing fish, lifted from the deep waters of the unconscious, converge on the center in a sprightly design based on a Celtic illumination.

Mandala 28

This mandala calls to mind an arrangement of nectar-filled vases, flowers, and incense given as votive offerings.

Mandala 29

Dynamic patterns frame an image of the Virgin Mary in this mandala based on a rose
window in the Cathedral of Our Lady, Freiburg, Germany.

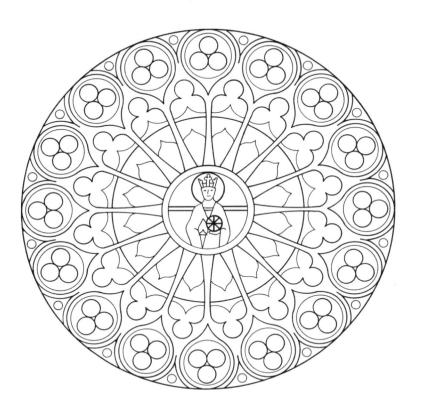

Mandala 30

The wheel demonstrates that balance is possible between the quiet, still center and the
quickly turning edge: each needs the other.

Mandala 31

This mandala was inspired by an eighteenth-century Nepalese design utilized as an aid in grasping the unity of self and cosmos.

Mandala 32

Discovering a standpoint in the midst of spiritual realization is one of the challenges we are given during the stage of Crystallization. Based on an Indian design.

Mandala 33

This mandala was inspired by an eighteenth-century Indian design invoking the goddess Tara, a bodhisattva who supports the quest for enlightenment.

Mandala 34

Petals spread out and out from the center, floating in the circular space of the mandala like a lily on a tranquil pond.

Mandala 35

Vigorously interweaving bands suggest the coursing energy of the universe in this mandala based on inlaid marble patterns at Emperor Akbar's tomb, Sikandra, India.

Mandala 36

Much of this complex design is comprised of a single strand, a visual teaching that the One and the many are the same. Inspired by designs at the tomb of Emperor Akbar.

Mandala 37

Curving lines glide smoothly over and under, toward the center and away, in this feminine mandala drawn from an Islamic design.

Mandala 38

A convoluted blossom fills the center of this mandala based on a sixteenth-century Iranian design.

Mandala 39

Moving your gaze along the complicated pathways in this mandala can be so confusing that thought surrenders and calm prevails.

Mandala 40

Nesting pairs rotate around each other and the center—wheels within a wheel.

Mandala 41

Just as naturally as planets orbit the sun, we experience the psyche's center of gravity as the Imago Dei, the inner Christ, the image of God within.

Mandala 42

A meditating figure seems at home in the universe, seated at the center of this mandala inspired by a Buddhist thangka, or scroll painting.

Mandala 43

Like atomic particles spinning matter into being, this mandala creates an image with lines that swirl. Do you see the six-pointed star formed by intersecting circles?

Mandala 44

Elegant circles intertwine, like dancers moving together in unison, attuned to the center—
and the Center—of the circle.

Mandala 45

Triangles merge to create diamonds, a symbol of the synthesis experienced during the stage of Crystallization.

Mandala 46

Pattern within pattern unfolds, alluding to the experience of deepening self-understanding.

Mandala 47

An extravagant blossom with transparent petals—all the better to let in the light.

Mandala 48

These winged circles await your colors to fully reveal the complexity of their relationships.

Mandala 49

Four ribbons intertwine to create a dazzling star with twelve points. Inspired by an Egyptian design.

Mandala 50

Odd numbers suggest energy, movement, and change. Even numbers connote balance, harmony, and completion. Forms defined by both types of numbers appear in this mandala based upon the numbers three, five, and ten. From an Islamic design.

Mandala 51

A vibrant matrix of lines reveals a serene pattern underneath—an agreeable paradox of movement and calm.

Mandala 52

Like holographic images of the center, smaller flowers take form within spaces defined by intersecting lines.

Mandala 53

During the stage of Crystallization, some experience understanding as resembling the discovery of a source of light within.

Mandala 54

In the traditions of Islamic art, straight lines are masculine in quality, while curved lines are feminine. Both are brought together here, weaving a balanced and tranquil pattern.

Mandala 55

As suggested by the hearts in this mandala, the resolution of differences during the stage of Crystallization releases unconditional love.

Mandala 56

Lines bound from side to side in the circle, creating almond-shaped spaces known as mandorlas. Within, a cosmic flower floats peacefully.

Mandala 57

A full-petaled flower yields up its ripe seeds, the quintessence of the stage of Crystallization.

Mandala 58

A blossom of fire holds back nothing from the blaze, a metaphor for living one's life to the fullest.

Mandala 59

A wisdom figure meditates among celestial spheres, radiant light, and sacred fires in this mandala of the stage of Crystallization.

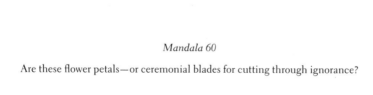

Mandala 60

Are these flower petals—or ceremonial blades for cutting through ignorance?

Mandala 61

Trumpet flowers grow from the center, sounding their messages through the colors you choose.

Mandala 62

Simple bands and fancy flowers happily achieve a balance in this Crystallization mandala. Based on a Turkish design.

Mandala 63

Triangles spin into labyrinths that amaze the eye. Drawn from an Islamic design.

Mandala 64

Plump berries nestle among the leaves and petals of this flowerlike mandala, conveying the
ripeness of the stage of Crystallization.

Mandala 65

The theme of divine union between active and receptive qualities can be found in this
delicate mandala inspired by an Islamic design.

Mandala 66

Even as we pause to reflect on the beauty of the design, the small crescent moons in this mandala are a reminder of the constancy of Nature's changes: the stage of Crystallization does not last forever.

Mandala 67

Twelve fish swim happily around the border of this mandala, a reference to the yearly turning of the cycle of time—slowed for a moment during Crystallization.

Mandala 68

The pure bands of a crystalline structure hold delicate flowers in place. Inspired by an Islamic design.

Mandala 69

This jewel-like mandala is based on a nineteenth-century Nepalese thangka used for clearing and focusing one's awareness.

Mandala 70

Arabesques of infinity signs, each one touching into the center, create vibrant patterns for coloring.

Mandala 71

What comes after a flower is done with blooming? The return to the earth, as foreshadowed by the withering edges of this mandala.

Mandala 72

The turning of the wheel reminds us of the ongoing nature of time and signals completion of our engagement with the lovely mandalas associated with Crystallization, a stage of the Great Round of Mandala. Inspired by a Buddhist stone carving.

Create your own mandala design!

Books by Susanne F. Fincher

Coloring Mandalas 1: For Insight, Healing, and Self-Expression

Coloring Mandalas 2: For Balance, Harmony, and Spiritual Well-Being

Coloring Mandalas 3: Circles of the Sacred Feminine

Coloring Mandalas 4: For Confidence, Energy, and Purpose

Creating Mandalas: For Insight, Healing, and Self-Expression

*The Mandala Workbook: A Creative Guide for Self-Expression, Balance, and
    Well-Being*

The Mini Mandala Coloring Book

Coloring for Balance: A Mini Mandala Coloring Book

Coloring for Insight: A Mini Mandala Coloring Book

Coloring the Sacred Feminine: A Mini Mandala Coloring Book